T0064499

INITIATION

Shining light on the sacred transitions of pregnancy, birth and motherhood, written by a mother for a mother

LAURA WIGHTON

BALBOA.PRESS

A DIVISION OF HAY HOUSE

Balboa Press books may be ordered through booksellers or by contacting:

Balboa Press
A Division of Hay House
1663 Liberty Drive
Bloomington, IN 47403
www.balboapress.com.au
AU TFN: 1 800 844 925 (Toll Free inside Australia)
AU Local: 0283 107 086 (+61 2 8310 7086 from outside Australia)

Print information available on the last page.

ISBN: 978-1-5043-2398-7 (sc)
ISBN: 978-1-5043-2399-4 (e)

Balboa Press rev. date: 12/17/2020

CONTENTS

FOREWORD

A book reserved for those mothers desiring to maintain foundations of spiritual, physical, emotional and mental well- being when ushering in new life.

This book can be read and used as a tool through any stage of pregnancy, birth, motherhood. Let the intentions of the words help to realign and guide you back to the sacredness of your journey.

This book encompasses deep, personal insights and also endeavours to speak of new evolutionary possibilities that pregnancy and motherhood could begin to offer new mothers. The book shares with you some practical tools and words of wisdom that can help influence you along into a more conscious and evolving journey. I hope you receive what your heart resonates with in joy and love.

When things seem tough, or too much let yourself have some time to remember the true purpose behind this initiation that is pregnancy and motherhood.

Written by a mother for a mother.

CHAPTER 1

HOW WE PERCEIVE PREGNANCY IN A MODERN WORLD VS A NEW PERSPECTIVE

The journey into pregnancy and motherhood is an initiation. This initiation can feel like a death of oneself. It can feel like you no longer exist and it creates a mourning for what once was. Women, often speak of feeling very vulnerable and confused during these times. Well, this is the common experience I have heard and unfortunately many miss out on the true opportunities that lie within the experience.

I am going to attempt to share with you a new perspective from my own personal experience of a wonderfully peaceful and empowering pregnancy and birth. This perspective may just help you embrace and enjoy your initiation and help you gain new levels of awareness and gratitude in order to show up for your babies, your family and yourself.

I will lead you through some mainstream thought processes that you may already be familiar with. As we have all been programmed to some degree to believe that pregnancy and birth are somewhat an inconvenience to the human experience. I will endeavour to help you change your mindset from one of fear to loving awareness.

The mundane routine and structure that humanity has created over the years has led us to a point where the modern lifestyle and chaos we have created is not conducive to such Initiations as pregnancy.

So, in order to be more accepting and open to the jewels that these initiations provide us with we need to begin to shift our consciousness and our lifestyles to line up with the sacred energy of pregnancy, birth and motherhood. This book may just help you to learn a few tools or new perspectives to integrate into your own life that will help you enjoy your experience, no matter what stage you are in.

During the period of pregnancy, a radical shift is occurring on a multitude of levels and it's a period of time for your body to morph. You may even revisit traumas, acknowledge your own shadows and learn to release control over situations, all of which are deeply confronting yet healing.

It is very easy to get overwhelmed by these internal and external changes and it's a common response for women to doubt their process. You may even start to fantasise over what once seemed familiar, but now lingers in the background of your mind as a past memory, keeping your attention in the past. I will touch on how this creates limiting thoughts and behaviours later in the book.

I've come to believe through my own personal experience that the actual reality in this mourning for familiarity of the life lived prior to pregnancy is only rooted in the fear of the unknown.

Fear being such a powerful force, once it is visited it can be hard to uproot and discard those fearful emotions and thoughts. So many women begin their journey of pregnancy and motherhood hand in hand with this fear. I have personally realised over the years that fear can be masked in so many areas of our life that we don't even know that it is the driving force.

The repercussions of deep-rooted fears intertwine themselves into all of your decisions and relationships. Resentment, anger, frustration, blame, lack of discipline, depression, these are the emotions that begin to rule our behaviours when stuck in a fear mindset.

Pregnancy is such a sacred time of transformation, when a woman is being used as a portal for life and is being asked to help change the narrative of humanity. Although, when she is rooted in fear Instead of harnessing her energy for her child she is handing over her energy to fear. Instead of receiving the gifts of the alchemist and transmuter of life with grace and strength, she is allowing her energy to drain out by giving her attention to the past and emotions of low vibration that keep her stuck in fear.

The story I have mentioned above, is a story that so many women experience. Nonetheless, it doesn't have to be your story. This story is part of a narrative you don't have to engage with or play any part of. Perhaps, you could even start to sew seeds of a different story and then begin to see this sacred journey in a different light.

For instance, you could begin to view this journey as an opportunity to evolve and change the narrative for your child. You could also view this time as an opportunity for you, the woman, the mother to transcend into greater heights of your true essence and bloom into your next faze of life easily and gracefully. I found this perspective to be so freeing and allowed me to walk more gracefully and confidently with my decisions throughout pregnancy and into birth.

If pregnancy was viewed as a sacred time of initiation into a woman's higher state of consciousness to prepare her for her greatest task and act of service to humanity. If this were the case then perhaps fear would no longer be the rooted energy a woman begins pregnancy with. Instead she could begin to feel empowered and connected with her body during this time, this was definitely the case for me.

With all of this considered, if the narrative were to be shifted from self and directed more to the bettering of humanities consciousness. Then, perhaps motherhood would be granted the importance it truly requires and society would be more accommodating and supportive to throughout this transition. I believe, this would eventually lead women to be more energised on their duties of motherhood and less focused on the past and lesser emotions.

CHAPTER 2

YOU MAY HAVE SOME QUESTIONS

Perhaps this new perspective may sound freshly invigorating to you if you are a new mother seeking more meaning and encouragement. Or perhaps this isn't so new to you. Either way is fine, I am not here to convince anyone, I am only interested in planting a seed that is dear to my heart, a seed that encompasses so much potency to me. So, if you have found yourself this far then perhaps it may be of some interest to you and perhaps you have a few questions circulating your brain.

Like;

Can this actually help a new mother experience more joy and autonomy throughout her pregnancy?

Can this perspective help me to view my role as a mother more honourably?

Will this help me to gain more confidence in the choices I make around pregnancy, birth and motherhood, even if they are alternative choices to the mainstream?

Can I gain more discipline and diligence around my motherly duties?

Does this shift give me more structure and purpose behind mothering?

Does this shift allow me to regain my energy in times of stress?

Does it allow for more time and space for my own practice of spiritual and wholistic wellbeing?

Does it ultimately help me regain confidence in my own innate intuition and does it allow me to trust in my child's being?

Well, I can only share with you from my own experience and response I have had from this shift in perspective and my experience screams YES to every one of those questions. I gained so much more awareness around how my role as a mother could not only benefit my child's life, but it can also benefit my own growth, and the future of humanity.

One thing that made itself aware to me throughout your own journey is that we are no longer in a time where knowledge is enough, we need to be proactive with the knowledge we gain. Learning how to maintain rooted in this new perspective, when so many of us are rooted in the past of limiting beliefs, negative mental patterns and unhealthy behaviours became the real goal at hand.

I realised that I had to get real, I had to have to release the old in order to make way for the new, and ultimately I had to learn to trust and have faith in myself and my baby.

We live in a modern world that is constantly bombarding our systems with over stimulation, new ideas, new products, new challenges and there are just so many triggers and so many habitual beliefs that can keep you slipping back and returning to old perspectives. With many of the benefits and advances that the modern world provides, there are also limitations.

And so, it is easy for us to get stuck and triggered into these limiting behaviours, even if you can intellectualise these concepts it can still be hard to fully embody the change.

In order to maintain these new perspectives and manifest real change in your life and your baby's life you need to learn how to proactively take the steps and maintain a strong foundation towards the change you wish to see.

I have come to witness that for most women the overwhelm of juggling this task along with all of the other thing's life demands of her gives little room for things like spiritual and wholistic self-care. I have learnt that when self-care isn't respected or taken into account, as a parent or a partner, you begin to burn out and negative emotions like resentment, anger, and frustration set in.

You must acknowledge as a woman, mother, partner, and friend, that self-care on all multitudes of levels should be taken seriously if you wish to show up in your life as the best version of yourself. That best version then ripples out and positively impacts the ones you love and care for.

CHAPTER 3

SELF-CARE, ROUTINE, AND DISCIPLINE, YOU AND YOUR BABY DESERVE IT

There is a silent elephant in the room, when we speak of pregnancy or motherhood, and sometimes not so silent. It's the expectation that as woman you must choose between motherhood and your own wellbeing. I believed this at first, especially being a young girl and witnessing my mother, my grandmothers, my aunties, all of which I loved and cared about. I was seeing them all neglecting and compromising their own worth, wellbeing, and self-care for other people in their lives.

Of course, they were only doing this from an act of what they thought and intended to be love. I have now come to see love and caring for others in a different light. In fact, I now know deep down within the deepest parts of my being that when a mother is fully aligned with her task as a mother she allows and priorities her own wellbeing as extremely important in order to complete her job as gracefully and attentively as possible.

Through my own experience, through my own childhood, through watching other mothers struggle and seeing the differences of wellbeing being expressed. I have come to realise that a large part of the challenge behind aligning motherhood and wholistic wellbeing is to do with the discipline of your mind.

Over the years I have come to see how the human mind can act as a friend or as a foe, it depends on your relationship with yourself. This includes your internal dialogue, how you speak about yourself to others, how you feel in your body, how you nourish or don't nourish your body. These are the elements that will determine the type of relationship you have with yourself.

Once a set of programs are repeated in your mind it is extremely hard to erase and change this internal dialogue. Hence, why a lot of people find it easier continuing life with the same mental dialogue that is rooted in fear versus taking the time to reprogram and change.

Although the challenge and enormity surrounding the task of reprogramming your own mind. It is still very achievable and rewarding in the long term to put in the time and effort to do so. As overwhelming as it may feel in the present moment, it is this effort that will help and assist you as a new mother on your journey and throughout motherhood.

During pregnancy a woman is not only gifted the chance to grow new life within, she is also given the chance to rest her body deeply, it's a great time to put away any excuses, put away the to do lists and just drop into your intuition and move throughout your day in a way that feels best to you. It's a time for deep rest and rejuvenation.

The 9 months gestational period is a beautiful time to truly grasp the internal and physical changes you're going through and all of the other changes that will come post-partum. In hindsight I can say that it was the rest during pregnancy that prepared me for the peak moments of birth.

As a mother, if you are willing then there also lies within this journey another hidden opportunity to renew and upgrade yourself on an energetic level. The human body holds within it every emotion from all past experiences, this can now be backed up strongly by the scientific community. Whether it be a childhood memory between you and a parent that encompasses negative emotion, an experience of humiliation you endured at school, or whether it be a trait or quality that holds you back.

Now is the time to relinquish its grip on you and free yourself. This period can hold grand healing potential for you as a mother and help you better prepare for the initiation that is to come.

If you allow yourself this opportunity to go within and release these shadow parts, parts that no longer serve you and allow gentle space for the healing work and reprogramming, then you are gifted extraordinary transformation. The transformation is the alchemy of transmuting fear into love and suddenly you will see these changes as empowering and you will embrace them with grace and excitement.

I want to clarify that, yes! I am shining a lot of light onto the magic and awe moments of pregnancy and motherhood, but this does not negate the trials and errors that you may experience as a mother. Like all areas of life, duality exists here too. The tiredness, the sacrifice, the mourning and grief of one's old life, the birth that didn't go to plan, the lack of support, the depression. Sure, these are all very real situations that some women experience.

I am not saying that these things don't have to exist at all, I am suggesting that if we shift our perspective, perhaps we can meet these challenges hand in hand with grace and love. You must never lose sight of the inner strength and endurance you as a mother are capable of.

CHAPTER 4

TRANSITIONING FROM MAIDEN TO MOTHER

As you transition from maiden to mother. If you can envision all of the women that have birthed before you and envision their energy surrounding you, envision the initiation they went through, the blood, sweat and tears. Hold this image in your mind's eye and never lose sight of this vision, keep the strength and grace as your backbone. Then, when you traverse through challenging times you will be held by this powerful force of your ancestors. You will find the strength and courage to continue with love and grace.

Our minds are like sponges and they're constantly observing and absorbing the information our environments transmit. The information downloaded from our environments into our subconscious is used to create programs that we eventually follow whether we are aware of it or not. Hence, the importance of us keeping guard and sorting through these mental files to get rid of the ones that do not serve us.

The transition period from maiden to mother was a pivotal time for me to eliminate old behaviours and thoughts that were no longer serving me. It was an extremely raw and real time, where I was forced to sit with a lot of old ways that I knew I didn't want to take forward with me as a mother.

I began to realise that to maintain this level of awareness of my mind and body and how I interacted with the world around me I needed to create sacred time and space for myself. I needed to return to the importance of the sacredness of this Initiation and devote more time for ritual and self-care. I believe that you too will revel in the difference this makes to your own personal journey.

If you do decide to integrate sacred time for self-care practices. During the time you put aside, whether it be a few minutes or hours you will begin to connect and strengthen your innate wisdom with the mental, physical, emotional and spiritual elements of your being. By doing so you are filling up your cup so to speak and reconnecting to source that will remind you of your task at hand and guide you back into your heart space.

None of this is intended for the ego, this is all deep heart work. It is easier for the ego to scream and shout when things get tough, to yell and expel negativity at loved ones to please itself. But to defuse heated emotion with love and grace is the work of an alchemist, it is the bi-product of someone who knows the work and knows the value of the task at hand.

This level of awareness and care into a mother's self should not be mistaken for ego but rather a devoted mother willing to evolve her consciousness, the consciousness of her own child and that of humanity.

When a woman traverses the depths of her soul, she is met with so many programs of fear and doubt that essentially are not hers but yet they are running her psyche. Pregnancy, in fact before pregnancy even begins if possible, is an integral time to reassess these programs and their place within your mind. You should really be asking yourself why am I allowing these programs to take up valuable space within my mind?

CHAPTER 5

HOW ARE SOCIETY'S PROGRAMS INFLUENCING YOU?

I use the term 'program' and I understand this word may be used loosely, so to really magnify in on what these programs are in terms of pregnancy and motherhood let me explain in further detail.

When the thought or the experience of pregnancy becomes a reality in a woman's life, what surfaces into her conscious mind are a lot of fears and scenarios. These fears, she has either heard or taken on through television advertisements, news channels, and other media outlets or even just stories of other people's negative experiences.

Once a program, so in this case a television advertisement that portrays pregnancy or childbirth in a negative light. Once this story has been processed by your mind it is deeply rooted within your mind and this is where your perspective begins to grow, from this fearful place. Did you form your perspective through your own experience? Or was this seed planted from external sources?

This is the exact cause of fear throughout pregnancy and birth and motherhood, this is where the self-doubt stems from. You as a mother innately know what is best for you and your child. With the right support, sacred space to heal old wounds, time to discard of limiting beliefs, fears and old programs you can achieve a peaceful and empowering birth.

From this place a mother is strong, a mother is confident, she is able and willing to journey through her initiation with fierce spiritual power. From this place a mother is in tune with her inner world, she is no longer draining her energy and giving her power over to external forces. Through my own experience on this path of initiation it became integral for me to protect my energy, to spend time alone processing and integrating.

It became very obvious to me especially as I got closer to the birth that a lot of people felt that in order to justify their own experience they had to verbally project that onto me. I learnt that I had to shield my emotional body and be very careful with how I navigated conversations with others.

Is this a negative thing? No. Of course other people are valid to share and express their own perspectives, but it is also extremely valid and important for you as a mother to protect yourself and be cautious of what is your own concern or worry and what is that of another.

During pregnancy you will find yourself extremely sensitive and receptive to the world around you, and so if you're someone who is already empathic to energy, then the need to protect your energy may be even more vital for you.

I have come to know many women who before endeavouring from maiden to mother were extremely diligent with health, self-care, and even made spirituality an integral part of their lives. Then after birth have come to forget, skip or neglect these factors in their own life. Allowing this to happen, allowing yourself to be so neglected and burnt out is not beneficial to you, your baby or the rest of your family.

This is something I have come to learn the hard way, being someone who is extremely self-dependant, sometimes to my own demise, I had to learn that asking for help isn't me failing, and that allowing my baby to be in the care of another you trust while you meditate, take a bath, or just take time to read a book, is ok.

Even beyond someone else lending a helping hand with my baby I realised that I had to become good at time management. That meant when my baby slept, I slept, or when she was content, I could manage to prepare dinner, do some writing for this book, make a phone call to a loved one or whatever else needed doing.

It meant that I had to adjust, I had to get up to speed with the changes that my life now demanded of me. If it weren't for taking a really good look within, and giving myself self-care when I needed it or asking for help, then I can admit things wouldn't have gone as smoothly.

CHAPTER 6

LEARNING TO TAKE CARE OF YOU, THE MOTHER

There is this notion that I have heard since I was young that women have to neglect themselves and only put their baby before them other-wise they are deemed selfish.

Of course, taking into consideration that your baby's needs have been met, then this is sometimes not true. Sometimes and a lot of the time you need to put yourself first, because if you aren't in your optimal then how are you going to be of service to others?

Along the journey I have heard so often from other mothers about their feeling of guilt. The feeling of guilt over the smallest things and hearing how this feeling affected them on an emotional level got me feeling quite concerned.

As mothers we can do a lot for our babies, we feed them and sustain them solely from providing milk from our breasts in the early months and years. We then also provide emotional comfort and love, they look up to us, they learn from us and to some point idolise and rely on us.

Somewhere along the way we then begin to lose ourselves in the caring of our babies, we begin to forget that the exact same needs we are providing for our babies we also need.

Too often I hear the stories of mothers saying they don't have time to eat, and that they get through the day on coffee or other stimulants. I hear the stories of mothers giving up spiritual practices, movement therapy and exercise become limited, simple hygiene neglected and hobbies, activities that bring them joy are forgotten or shrugged off as unimportant.

By letting go of these things we once deemed important to solely focus on our babies may seem like an act of service. Yet, by doing this we are actually doing a disservice to our babies, our families, friends and ultimately ourselves.

As I progressed along my own personal initiation into motherhood I began to realise the real goal was to create complete balance within my relating to my baby and my relating to myself. I realised that I couldn't go off track in either direction I had to continuously work on readjusting in order to find the balance.

So, some days looked like external giving and providing to baby, and other days my self-care and solitude needed to take priority but most days encompassed both. A good day had both baby time and me time, and through finding the sweet spot I began to ride this wave of symbiosis between loving on my baby and loving on myself.

It became clear that this old paradigm of full self-neglect in order to serve another had become redundant. I realised that I didn't have to jeopardise my own wellbeing in order to be a successful mother. In fact, it actually was of benefit to my entire family if I took pride in retaining a self-care and spiritual practice.

So, how did I manage to find this balance as a new mum? How did I manage to create a functional household and keep everyone happy including myself? I am so enthralled to share this because the more I speak with other mothers and observe the world around me the more I get this deep urge to share my perspective.

I literally have a visceral bodily response knowing that this advice, insight could somehow positively impact another mother's life. Or if not received instantly by the reader I know that this kind of thought process will be relative to the new paradigm shift we are collectively heading into.

CHAPTER 7

FINDING OUT I WAS PREGNANT, AND MY PEACEFUL PREGNANCY AND BIRTH

I remember the first moments I knew I was pregnant I remember feeling the energy flowing through my womb, and having a deep sense of responsibility that I now encompassed, even well before my sweet daughter joined us earth-side.

But it wasn't just a responsibility I felt within my immediate family It was something that united me with the entire world. It was a responsibility and an act of service to humanity that having my first child entailed.

It also felt like the most rewarding of all responsibilities I have ever had. I had played many roles within my community within this lifetime, but none had come to make as much sense as this one. Nothing could quite level up to the immense purging, growing and expanding as growing my own child within did, birthing her and then somehow managing to guide her consciously into a world that seems somewhat dishevelled.

In a time of such uncertainty, covid19, isolation, lockdown, distance from friends and family, family illness, threatening fires, global economic fragility, the list could go on.

I still felt that my child could not have come at a more appropriate time and this time made me feel somewhat indebted to raising a conscious child that believed within her core of a world that resembled peace, love and awareness.

Gradually, day by day, as my mind and body processed so much external grief of the world around me, I simultaneously learnt to transmute this grief into love and it was in these moments where I was viewing so much external demise that I learnt something.

I learnt that it doesn't matter too much about the external going on's of our world as it does about the state of our internal world. I began to then make the correlation about how too my experience of pregnancy and motherhood could also take on the same meaning.

Firstly, it seemed integral that I took time to simply be, in silence, usually by myself and usually immersed in a natural setting. The time of my pregnancy synced up with the time of us moving into a new house that happened to be smack bang in the middle of a national park. Surrounding our house were trees upon trees that painted their way over a mountain range. A creek also wrapped itself around the valley we were nestled in, and at any given opportunity I found myself down by the creek swimming and meditating by the water hole.

The sounds of the wildlife that also called this area home were comforting to me and I began to develop a strong relationship with my surroundings the more I allowed myself to simply be. This natural setting was a major help to me in developing a sense of stillness and calm as I traversed further into pregnancy. This period of time was transformational for me and integral as I transitioned from maiden to mother.

It was through being surrounded by so much nature and peaceful energy that I came to view this transition from maiden to mother as an 'Initiation'. I began to view this journey in a different light from what I was taught and from how I was seeing other mothers dealing with it. In fact, that's exactly how they were coping with it, just by 'dealing with it'. In a general sense this way of dealing with it encompassed a lot of detachment and a lot of heavy and negative energy.

I sensed other mothers living through their initiation with a lot of resentment, I saw them experience PTSD, post-partum depression and a lot sadness for their birth experience and journey not going to plan because they were not the ones making the decisions that they deep down wanted.

Instead of being the commander of their own ship, they seemed to be the ones handing over their power and then just dealing with how things panned out because they felt they had no other choice. It was as if they did not know that they held the power of the entire universe within them, as if someone else had a stronger insight into their world than they did.

Through these realisations I began to tune into my body and my mind and ask the questions of what I wanted for my pregnancy and birth and the more I listened to that the more confident I became in being the decision maker of my life. I knew that there was a world beyond my own intuition that could be of benefit to me if I needed the help, but it was really important to me that I firstly listened and trusted in my own intuition and frankly I am so glad I did.

Days turned into months and before I knew it I was full term and had not undergone any outside intervention, no tests, scans, needles, no seeing of what gender lied within, just trust and a deep sense of awe for the being growing inside my womb. At first, outsiders and family members passed judgement, expressed their own worries and concerns but nothing could change my mind.

By the time I had reached full term I was fully charged with confidence and knowing that my baby and I were going to finish our journey with her in my arms in the peace and serenity of our home. I had made the decision from the very beginning that I was going to birth my baby at home and so I spent the entire 9 months envisioning and visualising this birth and it was the most transformational experience to see this plan come to fruition.

To have spent the entire 9 months growing my baby and then birthing her in the same environment without any intervention. At first, this seemed like a story far away from possible. I had created this notion in my mind from years of programming from outside influence and if it weren't for my determination and trust in my own intuition then perhaps it wouldn't have played out this way.

After journeying through pregnancy and now birth and seeing the full potential of my mind, body and spirit it became even clearer to me that most of us are living our lives from a place of fear which is limiting to our evolution and experience in this lifetime.

Perhaps I had not given my intuition the trust and perhaps I had been scared into fear from the stories of others. If this were the case then perhaps the outcome and experience of my birth may not be one I can stand proudly in. Perhaps my experience into motherhood would be tampered by trauma and regret like the stories of so many other women.

I share my insight and experience of what so many deem as a radical and raw birth not to make anyone else's story feel less than but to share a story of inspiration and empowerment for other mothers who wish to gain deeper connection and trust in their own mind and bodies.

The experience of my pregnancy right up until birth was one of peace and love and to be completely honest it was so rejuvenating on so many levels. It not only created a safe habitat for my baby to develop within but it also simultaneously provided a safe environment for me, the mother, to ascertain a deeper connection with myself and align with a vision of birth that I deemed to be nurturing.

My experience not only provided growth for myself, but to have my partner and my mother witness me travel through pregnancy and to be present at the birth was extremely empowering for them too. They were both in awe at the experience and they too could feel the wonder of birthing my child in the comfort of my own home.

CHAPTER 8

MOTHERHOOD AND A PERSPECTIVE ROOTED IN EVOLUTIONARY GROWTH.

Throughout the pregnancy I kept my mind's eye focused on the bigger picture. Knowing that the 9 months gestational period would go by quickly I wanted to prepare myself mentally for the massive transition I would experience once my baby was in my arms. To do this, I often would mediate on the idea of my child being a child of their own destiny, and that my role in their journey once they arrived was to provide a safe, loving and nurturing environment that would help them develop into their own spirits essence.

I would picture my child as they developed into their personality and I pictured them expressing to me their desires. In this moment I remembered how when I was their age, I too had my own desires, quirks and sense of self and remembered how hurtful it was to not have the acknowledgement or acceptance for who I was by the people around me. This helped me realise this was not a feeling I ever wanted my child to feel.

Through revisiting these emotions from my childhood I was able to see the pure innocence and individual essence of every child and it brought me to a sense of acceptance for my child before I could pass any judgement on their individual nature.

Before I had even met my baby, I was already experiencing strong emotions of acceptance and unconditional love.

My perception on my role as a parent was completely conflicted with the mainstream idea of parenting. I was no longer streaming through this journey with the idea of corrupting or changing my child's nature. Rather I was here to be of service to them and the world around me.

Of course I am here to guide and provide a strong foundation for my child that helps them respect themselves and others as they grow to develop relationships. I believe that as parents we are here to play a part in our child's life and teach them morals and values and continue to offer support and guidance. Although, we are not in their lives to try and change them, control them or supress their true nature.

As I look around at society this is where I see parents confusing guidance with control. As children get older and turn into adults their responsibility for their actions becomes solely theirs and as parents our impact lessens. So, I have come to realise that in order for me to gain respect and teach respect to my child I need to encompass a level of freedom and individuality into our relationship.

As I am still new into motherhood, my baby currently being 5 months old. I don't want to sound as if I have everything figured out or that I am telling any mothers what to do. I am merely just sharing my own personal insight into how I have navigated these early months and the mindset I have as I continue further into motherhood. For me this realisation of giving my child their freedom of person and autonomy just seems so natural for their personal growth and I really look forward to honouring that as time moves on.

What I do really want to elaborate on further though is the idea of pregnancy and motherhood being an opportunity for personal evolutionary growth, mind, body and soul. Through adapting this mindset in my own journey. I began to not take things so personally, I began to find more gratitude in the hard and confusing times, and I began to honour all of the cycles and stages with reverence. This mindset helped me stay close to love rather than being thrown of course into fear.

In my personal life I had a lot of noise and stress that was going on externally both personally and on a global level but I never allowed the noise to penetrate into my vortex. I was completely indebted to staying focused on my own wellbeing and the wellbeing of my growing baby.

Although, this external noise could have been deemed as quite stressful, I am grateful for the contrastive nature as it helped me to continue to see that I always have a choice in regards to how I react to any given situation.

Any moment that stress began to appear outside of my vortex I reminded myself that this is not my noise to handle, my priorities are my wellbeing and that of my baby. I understand that stress has become somewhat of a normal occurrence for most people. But I want to remind you that you do not have to take on excess stress and you have the right to not play apart in any other personal or global stresses that put you out of balance.

At first, this was a really hard thing for my mind to grasp and then to also put it into practice. I grew up learning that saying yes all of the time even if it jeopardises your own wellbeing is ok. I am also glad that I have reached a point in my life where I can now listen to my own internal compass and say no if something doesn't feel right. I am telling you that although it is uncomfortable at first there is so much freedom and relief in listening to your gut feeling and honouring your own wellbeing first.

In fact, the moment I started saying no, the moment I began to honour my intuition was the moment that my family life began to truly flourish, it was the moment that my relationship with my partner began to delve deeper, communication was more available, I was more present with myself and my baby and I also noticed an ease and calm that flooded my being. It was a sensation that replaced this background anxiety I had been feeling for so long without even being consciously aware of it.

I began to feel more confident in asking for space or asking for help from my partner or close friends, without this heavy feeling of guilt. I also noticed that I became less reactive and more accepting of what was, I had more time for other people's differences and I wasn't so caught up on what others were doing. Instead, I was more invested in my own family life. This feeling is so important to me, my family life is so important to me and so to honour that without the feelings of guilt or shame was a massive relief.

The energy I had been putting into these lesser emotions I was now investing into my own personal wellbeing. I began to study again and completed my reiki master's course so smoothly. The feeling of confidence and alignment that came with that completion, gave me strength and a creative energy to pursue projects I had only been dreaming of before.

I was also now taking time to sit in deep mediation from 5 to sometimes 20 minutes, twice a day. This practice became so beneficial and impacted my family life greatly, especially with a new baby on board. During these mediations my thought processes became more coherent, I was able to envision plans and ideas more clearly. When I would finish up a meditation my mind was calmer and clearer and I was more able to plan and organise my day.

Another tool I used was writing down affirmations and speaking them out aloud or in my mind. During pregnancy and before the birth this tool was extremely helpful, every night before bed I would read my birth mantra that I had created and I believe this truly helped with my peaceful birth.

Writing down affirmations became second nature to me, and the more I did it the more I wanted to write in general. Soon, I began writing down more descriptive words that expressed how I wanted to feel or how I was feeling, that then lead to writing down more detailed descriptions about future plans I was curating. Before I knew it, all of these tools were supporting one another so beautifully and they then became a step by step process for me.

I would sit in meditation, create space in ln mind, write down affirmations, speak them aloud, sit in meditation, I would have visions come to me, or desire arise, I would then journal about them, express how they made me feel in detail, meditate, take small steps in making the desires come to life, and the cycle would continue.

This continual cycle helped assist me in preparing for birth in a calm and peaceful way, by the time birth came around I was so ready. In fact, the birth itself didn't seem like a separate event to the pregnancy, it flowed seamlessly and I was able to keep the same energy throughout.

It was through pregnancy that I actually developed a much more dedicated spiritual practice. In hindsight, it was actually the slowing down and removing of guilt and shame that truly allowed this all to happen. Allowing myself the time and space for practice was integral and I now know that it is the same formula I am going to rely on throughout the rest of my motherhood journey and life in general.

CHAPTER 9

SHIFTING YOUR PRIORITIES

I understand that life is busy, there are many commitments and roles we play and the amount of responsibility we bear as mothers is huge. But, at the same time we need to begin to access what our priorities are, sometimes a shifting of priorities is do-able and we can manage to regain balance easily. Other times it is a massive life shift, and a rearranging of every aspect of our lives can seem daunting or unrealistic but sometimes this drastic change is exactly what your soul desires in order to function at its highest potential.

Again, this is such a personal subject, and I am going to leave that up to you. Although, my guess is that if you've found yourself this far into my book then there is a part of your soul that is in resonance with my words and perhaps this change is also a part of your destiny.

Pregnancy, birth, motherhood none of these are for the faint hearted. In fact, these challenges are incredibly testing at times. That is why I have shifted my mindset into viewing them as an 'Initiation' because each step of the way you're constantly learning so much about yourself and the world around you.

You go through a cycle of death, rebirth, upgrade, death, rebirth, upgrade and in between each stage there are losses and gains. It's exactly how the natural world works and yet some-how we have been programmed to become so detached from these cycles.

We have created a world that does not support these natural cycles for women. The stage from maiden to mother is incredibly beautiful and miraculous yet young women are not taught or supported by the world at large. In fact, pregnancy for so long has been viewed as a sort of hindrance to a woman's life, as if everything else comes before this journey. So, women continue to journey through pregnancy and birth alone and in shame without the proper guidance they so deserve.

Can you imagine if young women had the knowledge and support before, during and after these initiations? Wow, it would completely change the narrative of humanity, don't you think? Children would be born in honour and peace. We would be raising children that know how to honour themselves and the world around them. Women would be flourishing in grace and joy after birth, they would be present with their babies without the heaviness that so many women experience post-partum.

This is why I am writing with such conviction, this is why I am writing at all, because I have experienced it first-hand. I have experienced the effects of what integrating a spiritual and wholistic self-care practice into my life looks like. I have experienced a peaceful pregnancy. I have experienced an empowering free birth in my own home surrounded by loved ones. I have experienced care and nurture post-partum and I am continuously seeing the effect of this practice as I traverse further into motherhood and my family life.

If you receive any wisdom from this book at all I hope you know that you are important and just because you are bearing another life, does not mean you have to neglect your own wellbeing.

With this being said I encourage you, mother, take more time to strengthen your spiritual practices. Whether it be daily movement like; dance, walking, running, swimming, or meditation, journaling, reading out aloud affirmations, practicing deep presence, eating nourishing food. It doesn't really matter about the form it takes place. It just matters that you deepen your connection with your inner world. Before making decisions check in with yourself and see if those choices really resonate. Remember that through strengthening these practices, you're not losing time, you're actually gaining time and you actually get a lot clearer on your priorities and task/time management of your life.

I truly believe that if you do this you will actually see your relationships flourish. Especially the one with yourself, which in turn impacts every other element of your life. I only say this with confidence because I have seen the changes within my own life through implementing these tools.

Your initiation in to pregnancy, birth and motherhood can be; seamless, freeing, joyous and peaceful. It is up to you how you wish to direct your energy and it is up to you to put in the time and effort if you truly wish to have a more wholistic and enriched experience. I now can see that the more we tune into how sacred this experience is, the more sacred it becomes every step of the way.

I don't expect that your journey be the same as mine, although I do hope your journey is being created by you. I do hope that you are the primary decision maker and that you are confident and happy with your decisions.

It is through my own personal Initiation that a seed within me has grown. It is a seed that can be watered by many women all over the world. Through this seed of new perspective being felt within your heart, we can begin to grow closer to a world that outside of us is beautiful, inspiring and consciously created by us as captains of our own ship.

I believe the future is bright because I can firstly feel it within, just like I felt the desire for a peaceful pregnancy and birth, too I feel the desire for a world that I know my child will flourish in. I believe if you too can hold this perspective in your mind's eye, and continue to work on your own wholistic wellbeing then you can begin to relish in the bounty that this sacred initiation offers you.

In the following pages I have included some Affirmations for you to practice incorporating into your journey, no matter what stage you are in these will be relevant. I have also included many prose style insights I wrote to help inspire and uplift you during more challenging times.

I hope that my intentional words of wisdom can rest in your hearts knowing that you have the power of your destiny and you too can experience a calm, peaceful and joyous Initiation into your journey.

AFFIRMATIONS

"I am capable of letting go,
I am capable of surrendering
into the experience
I am capable of trusting my body
I am capable of pleasure I
am capable of Joy
I am capable of softening into pain
I am capable of transmuting
my fears into love
I am capable of birth."

-LW

"I am confident in my ability to
love my growing body
I am confident that my body
will nourish and protect my
baby throughout pregnancy
I am confident in the
process of pregnancy
I am confident in my decision to birth
my baby how I choose
I am confident in the transformations
that will take place mentally,
physically & spiritually
I am confident in my new baby
and in the new me."

-LW

"I trust in my own inner instincts to
mother
and care for my child
I trust in my design for parenting
and raising my child with an
open mind and heart
I trust that my journey into mothering
will teach me all the valuable lessons
I need to grow and evolve
I trust that my child will also evolve
and grow into the conscious being
that he/she so desires to be
I trust that Love/ Compassion
& Respect will always be at the
heart of our relationship."

-LW

"I am strong in my mind
I am strong in my body
I am strong in my spirit
I am strong in my hearts knowing
I am strong in my ability to trust
I am strong in my ability to achieve
I am strong in my energy
I am strong in my discipline
I am strong in my love
I am strong in my will
I am strong in my faith
I am strong in my journey."

-LW

"I am led by my own intuition
I am in tune with my inner guidance
I am in sync with what is right for
me and my baby I am protected
from negative influences
I am easily in flow with my
heart's desires
I am strong in my knowing
I am strong in trusting my
inner guidance
I am in alignment with what will serve
me and my baby best
I am strongly attuned to the
best-case scenario at all times thanks
to my
own inner guidance."

-LW

"I am love
I speak with love
I act in love
I am love
I set intentions in love
I pray in love
I am love
I grow my baby in love
I birth my baby in love
I am love
I am love
I am love"

-LW

"I am strong enough to create order
and peace in my life
I am strong enough both in my mind
and in my actions
My mental, physical and spiritual
well-being are important for the overall
health of my child and I
Ritual, routine and structure
will be the backbone of my
successful mothering journey
I will not be overwhelmed by the
grandness of this task
I will be prepared, centred and
organised at all times."

-LW

"Lightness fills my mind
Ease flows through my body
Each cell vibrating harmoniously
My neck loosens
My shoulders release
I breathe deep into my womb
My heart beat matching my breathe
Tension leaving my body
A smile naturally appearing
Here I am
I've arrived home
Back to my centre
Back to grace"

-LW

"I am gentle on my mind
The thoughts I choose to use are kind
I am gentle on my body
I consume foods that nourish
and hydrate my body
I am gentle on my spirit I
use ritual, affirmations and
gratitude to help me ascend
I am gentle because my health and my
baby require me to be
I am gentle because it is what feels good"

-LW

"I am letting go of all that
does not serve me
I am free from past limitations
I am comfortable in the unknown
I am merging into a new being
I am safe and secure in this transition
I am accepting of all parts of me
I acknowledge and release
generational trauma`
I work daily towards healing
these parts of me
I am doing the work now for the future
of my
child and my future self."

-LW

"I am full of power
I am focused I am filled
with energy to pursue
I am unstoppable
I am willing
I am self-sufficient
I am sure of myself
I am sure of my abilities
I am confident I am able I am capable
I am determined."

-LW

"I know that my potential lies beyond
the limitations, beyond the labels and
beyond the roles I play
I know that I am capable of achieving
things above and beyond the expectations
people and I place upon myself
I know that how I show up
outside of these roles also impacts
how I show up as mother
I know that I have a well of
information and inspiration within
me that holds far greater importance
than anything outside of me
I know I am of this earth
and beyond this earth."

-LW

"I am giver of life
I am a sacred vessel of infinite potential
I am mother
I am a seeker
I am a teacher
I am mother
I am an alchemist of the stars
I am a healer of the earth
I am mother
I am a channel of light
I am a student of life
I am mother"

-LW

"Child, you are your own
Child, you are pure universal energy
Child, your love is pure
Child, you are here to teach me
Child, you have no limitations
Child, your essence is yours to express
Child, I will be here to guide you
Child, I will be here to nourish you
Child, I will be here to celebrate you."

-LW

"I am connected to all living things
I am a reflection of all
people on this planet
I am responsible for my interactions
I am in an energetic exchange with all
people
I come in contact with
I am bound to this earth by
earthly and celestial forces
I am as another is
My relationships are integral to how
my spirit plays out
I am aware of all of my relationships and
respect them and their roles in my life
I am grateful for all connections both
tangible and intangible."

-LW

"This Pregnancy is sacred
I honour the sacredness of
the entire experience
Each day I wake and relish in the
miracle that is growing within me
I am grateful from the very
core to be on this journey
I will carry gratitude forward into my
birthing experience and
into motherhood
I see the sacredness
I feel the sacredness
I honour the sacredness."

-LW

"I am devoted to the heart
I am devoted to healing on all levels
I am devoted to my daily practice
I am devoted to learning from life itself
I am devoted to being present with life
I am devoted to being the
best version of myself
I am devoted to being
present with my child
I am devoted to learning from my child
I am devoted to growing with my child
I am devoted to doing the work
I am devoted to loving
I am devoted to evolving."

-LW

"I am filled with a well of energy
My heart will always help sustain me
I am beyond this physical form
I am sure that there are higher
forces supporting me
I am capable of enduring
I am able to see the light at
the end of the road
I am well equipped with strength, vitality
and infinite energy to see me through
I am guided and supported by love
I know that the pain of birth is nothing
to fear but something to breathe into."

-LW

"I am aligned with my higher self
I express from a place of authenticity
My heart leads my mind
What I speak of is in alignment
with my actions
I only speak of truth
I embody my true essence
I partake in ritual each day
I am proactive in doing the work so that
I embody my truth
My inner world projects my outer world."

-LW

WISDOM

"Each day I wake with gratitude
Gratitude to fill my heart
and re-centre my being
This gratitude ripples out and positively
affects my child's life
Each day I work little by little on
healing past wounds, suppressed
emotions and trauma
I release energy through movement,
ritual, meditation and any practice
that helps shift the energy
Each day I work on bringing more
awareness, presence, and joy into my life
I choose to be proactive in my
healing and sit with all feelings
Each day I heal little by little."

-LW

"Your strength is not determined
by how many times you break,
It is how you build yourself back up
again, and again, time after time.
Your true strength is at the
heart of your willingness,
Your willingness to be ok with not being
ok and then rise again like a phoenix
Until your energy is no longer
stuck in the breaking down of the
self but instead it is rooted in the
rebuilding and regeneration phase."

-LW

"Love is always worth fighting for and darling this journey you are on is the biggest test of love you will find Love is never too much, and to recalibrate back into love is never too much effort. You will be tested beyond measure. You will almost believe you don't want love anymore Until you realise that this love is what is keeping you going Until you realise this love, you couldn't possibly live without. This love is always worth fighting for."

-LW

"This journey is no mistake, it is no random act of human doings. It is a planned and destined journey that has been organised and integrated meticulously. It has taken the entire universe to align so that this being of light can come through. Although, the human mind will try to dictate such unfolding's. Don't be doubtful that the time could not be more perfect. The human going on's are secondary to what the universe has already written for you."

-LW

"Pregnancy is a vulnerable
time You will be trying to navigate death
and rebirth of yourself as a new mother,
As well as navigating the judgement and
expectations of others on how you will
journey through and raise your child.
Don't allow the opinions of others to
determine your choices on how you will
show up. Allow your inner compass to
guide and direct you on your personalised
journey. As your body slows down during
the gestational phase, use this time to
strengthen your intuition and get to
the root of who you are and allow your
choices to come from
this sacred place."

-LW

"Ground yourself in your intuition, let it be the root that binds you to what feels right for you. Let it be the guiding force that ushers you back to your own discernment, so that you can find clarity through your own mind and heart. Take time and space for you. Allow yourself to be in your own energy. To strengthen and tone. To be and see. What is right for you and your baby. Don't be deterred by the words or opinions of outsiders. Let it wash over you with ease. Trust your intuition and trust your baby."

-LW

"As you journey further into your pregnancy you find yourself nearing more uncertainty. Pregnancy and birth do that, they destroy everything you've known before and test your trust in the unknown They will rip apart all pre-conceived ideas. Thoughts surrounding who you are and who you once were become so distant and vague, that you have no choice but to surrender and rebuild yourself. As scary as this process may seem to you, you must surrender, there will be beauty in your decay. Just know this is apart of the process, it's a necessary cleaning of the slate."

-LW

"Dear child of mine,
Growing so effortlessly
within, Thank you.
Thank you for my growing body, as it
represents our evolution together as one.
Thank you, for the endless kicks and
pokes day in and day out, they remind
me of your presence until the day come's
I hold you in my arms. Thank you, for
the marks you will lay upon my body,
they will continuously remind me of the
depths I traversed and limits I exceeded to
bring you earth-side. Dear child of mine,
thank you, for showing me my strength."

-LW

"Let me tell you now mumma,
you will want to cry, you may even
feel anger, perhaps even rage.
The overwhelm will have emotions
running at an all time high.
Know that this is ok.
You are adjusting, re-calibrating,
and stepping into a world of
newness that may seem foreign.
So take some time and cry if you need to.
Just know that all change and
things of grand importance take
an element of endurance.
Know that you have an infinite
well of power swirling within you.
Know that this too shall pass.
Know that there will be lighter
and sweeter days ahead."

-LW

"Walk with your head held high
Speak with a voice of confidence.
Wear your decisions and heart
on your sleeve Why? Because
darling you are a warrior.
You are worthy of such a title Because
you have proven your strength.
You have endeavoured through 9
months of growing life within and
now to birth your child earth side.
You deserve to be seen, heard and
honoured in all of your bounty.
You deserve to feel and embody this
power You are a warrior You are mother."

-LW

"Pregnancy and birth
will transform you, for some this
transformation may be more painful.
For some they may struggle to
see the necessity in the decay
before the blossoming.
If this pain is overwhelming for you, this
is your reminder to breathe into the pain.
Lean into the discomfort and work
out where it is rooted and why you are
holding on so tightly to the past.
Perhaps it is a program from childhood
that is rooted in comfortability
or it is a program that is set to
default in your reactions.
Whatever it may be, know that its
importance is no longer relevant
and that this journey you are on
surpasses all past programming."

-LW

"It will be detrimental to
your own evolution as well as your
child's to continue to make space
for ritual, meditation, intention
setting, and any form of practice
that grounds and centres you.
Whether it be the morning, the middle
of the day or the evening, whatever works
for you is when you should make time
and space for these sacred practices.
Use this time to fill up your cup,
re-energise and work towards
returning with your highest self.
These times will be pivotal for your
essential growth in order to deal with the
ever changing times of motherhood.
You have to make time for self-
development and self -nourishment
in order to show up as the
best version of yourself."

-LW

"Don't let the temporary struggle determine the rest of your experience with your child. There will for sure be days of complete haze and confusion but they are minor in the grander scheme of things. This among all other experiences in your motherhood journey are opportunities to evolve, hidden lessons lie within all hardships. So be easy on yourself, on those days that are hard, rest, take it slow and allow yourself space to breathe within the demands. Remind yourself daily, that this experience is more than just a physical one-dimensional experience. Instead it is an experience asking for your mental, spiritual, physical, and emotional growth in order to change the narrative of this planet."

-LW

"Over the horizon awaits a world that will bring humanity to a higher consciousness. It's a world that will bring forth new systems and new ways of living that align with a greater awakening. But first, we are being asked to rid ourselves of the old ways, the old thought patterns, the old limitations. In order for us to step into this new earth formation, we need to individually step up and do the work in order to heal and transcend. Our parenting approach and our children will be the catalysts for this new earth change. Let's allow our children to guide us into these new ways of being."

-LW

"Your journey as mother is uniquely
yours to experience and it should be a
reflection of you and your child's desires.
If you're on this journey as an evolving
mother who wishes to expand her
consciousness and her experience as
mother. Then, you probably want
to ask yourself some questions.
Am I coming from a place
of love or fear?
Are my intentions rooted
in ego or evolution?
Is this going to be of benefit to
me and my child's growth?
By asking these questions before reacting
to someone or something, we can realign
our core values with our external world."

-LW

"Our children are here to
help us grow.
They come into this world smaller and
more pure than us, but they hold so
much wisdom for us to learn from.
They will reflect back to us all of the
parts we have not healed yet, they will
hold us accountable for our baggage.
Our children will help us grow through
all of the uncomfortable moments so
that we can reach our fullest potential.
They are wise beyond their years,
and when we connect deeply and
give them our undivided attention
they show us this wisdom and they
communicate their needs quite clearly.
It is not the child that needs the
work done, it is the parent who
will be taught the grandest lessons
in life through the child."

-LW

"This life brings you closer
to the beginning.
Although we're told we near the end
the older we get, it's as if we actually
gain more insight as to who we are,
and we return to our perfect state.
This perfect state can be seen
in a newborn baby.
When the time comes when you
hold your baby in yours arms
and you gaze into their eyes.
You'll see the completeness and this is
the state in which we all return to.
We are whole and if we can see this
wholeness in our children's eyes then
we can nurture and support them as
a complete being rather than trying
to control or change them."

-LW

"Sometimes you will feel like
falling to the wayside but you will
again remember the immense purpose
that lies within this journey.
You will remember the stare of your
child's gaze erases all the sleepless nights.
You will remember that by you staying
focused on the larger picture of everything
that you can continuously return to
gratitude no matter the circumstance.
Deep connected breathe, meditation,
reduced stimulation, conscious
ritual of any sort can help bring
you back to your heart centre.
It's important to always come from this
place as it helps us see the love in all
situations, and helps us to be grateful for
what we have, whilst simultaneously re-
energizing our stamina
to deal with life."

-LW

"It is through your conscious awareness,
and your willingness to project your
energy into your life that will transform
and manifest the life you desire.
In saying this, the way you choose to show
up each day will impact how you and your
baby function in your dynamic of life.
Because, each thought, each word
spoken, each interaction, how you
hold yourself, every little energetic
vibration has a ripple affect into the
greater field of consciousness.
So choose wisely how you use your energy,
and this will not only greatly affect your
motherhood, but also your entire life."

-LW

"We've been led to believe that energy comes from external sources, coffee, other people's encouragement, sugar, food, etc; yet the true energy, the true source comes from within. It comes from the state of your mind. How well you are taking care of your inner landscape, will determine how prepared you are for this journey. If you can nourish your mind, the rest will follow.
Of course, movement of the physical body is important, and eating nourishing food will benefit you. But when those things aren't enough, when you've run yourself dry, having the skills of inner nourishment through will power, inner talk, calmness and a positive state of mind. These are the things that will help you to realign with your heart and get you through with grace."

-LW

"As a mother, the greatest gift you can give yourself and your child is to embody with confidence your truth. Who are you? What is the essence behind your actions? and How do you work towards achieving your day? These are questions you can ask yourself. As leaders, teaches, and role models, every action, every word we speak carries out a vibration and greatly impacts our children's lives. By bringing more awareness, presence and deep meaning into our lives we can help present ourselves in a clear and positive way that will benefit our children's growth. This sense of peace, confidence and clarity is what our children crave to feel safe and secure and confident in themselves."

-LW

Mother, never forget your importance, it is
through the recognition of your own needs,
it is through the healing of your own pain,
that you will then be a better mother.
By showing our children how to do the work,
how to heal and how to present and aware.
This is how we will create a new
earth. This is how we create a safer,
more joyous world for children.
May my words be received by your heart
in the way that you need to hear.
May they be a guiding force, or a lifting
message for you in times of doubt.
Mother, you are more than capable.
You are superhuman, and you are
Mother, wear your title confidence,
and know your worth.

-From one mother to another